LIZARDS

A TRUE BOOK®

by
Trudi Strain Trueit

Children's Press®
A Division of Scholastic Inc.

New York Toronto London Auckland Sydney
Mexico City New Delhi Hong Kong
Danbury, Connecticut

A banded
gecko

Reading Consultant
Nanci R. Vargus, Ed.D.
Assistant Professor
Literacy Education
University of Indianapolis
Indianapolis, IN

Content Consultant
Joseph T. Collins
Director, The Center for North
American Herpetology
Lawrence, KS

Dedication:
For Bailey, an explorer at heart

The photograph on the cover
shows a Jackson's chameleon.
The photograph on the title
page shows a green iguana.

Library of Congress Cataloging-in-Publication Data

Trueit, Trudi Strain.
    Lizards / by Trudi Strain Trueit.
        p. cm. – (A True book)
    Includes bibliographical references and index.
    ISBN 0-516-22651-7 (lib. bdg.)   0-516-29351-6 (pbk.)
    1. Lizards—Juvenile literature. [1. Lizards.] I. Title. II. Series.
QL666.L2 T764 2003
597.95—dc21
                                                                2002005878

Contents

Land of Lizards   5

Special Senses   8

Lounging Lizards   13

From Geckos to Komodos   20

Stay Away!   29

A Place in the World   39

To Find Out More   44

Important Words   46

Index   47

Meet the Author   48

A water monitor
in southeast Asia

Land of Lizards

Lizards have crawled on Earth for more than 200 million years. Lizards wriggle up trees in the rain forests. They perch like statues on desert rocks. The only places lizards are not found are the North and South Poles. It is too cold for lizards to live there.

A yellow-headed collared lizard perching on a desert rock

Lizards belong to a group of animals called reptiles. Snakes are also reptiles. More than four thousand different kinds of lizards live on our planet. Geckos, skinks, iguanas (ig-WAN-uhs), and monitors make up some of the main families of lizards.

A Great Plains skink

Special Senses

Every lizard has a head, a body, and a tail. Lizards also have eyes and ridged jaws. Most types of lizards have outer ears.

Most lizards have four legs, but a few kinds have two legs, and some have no legs at all. The glass lizard looks just like a snake—until it blinks. Snakes

Most lizards, such as the Agama lizard (left), have outer ears. Some lizards, such as the glass lizard (below), have no legs at all.

do not blink, but lizards usually do. Lizards can blink because they have movable eyelids. Snakes have only clear scales over their eyes called brilles.

A Tokay gecko cleaning its brilles with its tongue (above) and a chameleon looking in two different directions at once (right)

Some lizards, such as geckos and night lizards, have brilles too. A gecko will lick its eyes with its tongue to keep its brilles clean.

Lizards have good eyesight. Geckos have the best vision of

any lizard. The common chameleon (cah-MEAL-yen) can move each of its eyes separately. One eye may look forward to hunt for insects while the other eye looks backward for signs of danger. In less than one second, the chameleon can snap its long, sticky tongue out to catch an insect.

Larger lizards rely on their tongues for taste and smell. When a lizard's tongue flicks out of its mouth, it picks up samples of the air. The tongue

then touches two holes in the
roof of the lizard's mouth
called the Jacobson's organs.
They help the lizard tell what
objects and animals are nearby
by detecting their scents.

Lounging Lizards

Lizards spend a lot of time relaxing on tree branches, rocks, or sand. Lizards are **ectothermic** (eck-tuh-THERM-ick), which means "outside heat." They must depend on their **environments** to heat and cool their bodies.

To get warm, a lizard **basks** in the sun. The sun's heat gives

A sand monitor basking in the sun (left) and a desert spiney lizard resting in the shade (below)

the lizard energy to move and hunt. To cool its body, a lizard must rest in the shade. Many lizards can lighten or darken their skin to help them absorb more or less heat.

Lizards have skin made of thick, overlapping scales. The scales are made of **keratin**—the same thing that's in your finger-nails. Some lizards' scales have bits of bone in them. The bone acts as armor and adds strength to the scales.

In order to grow, a lizard must shed the top layer of its skin. This is called molting. The

A green anole lizard molting

clear, thin layer of skin may slide off all at once or in patches here and there.

Insects are the main meal for most lizards. Some lizards, such as green iguanas and basilisks, eat only plants. Gila monsters prefer reptile eggs and bird eggs. Larger lizards may eat

An iguana eating part of a cactus (above) and a Nile monitor lizard eating fish (right)

small birds, animals, and other lizards.

Lizards do not need to eat very often. A bird eats as many insects in one day as a lizard gulps down in a whole month.

The male carpet chameleon (at right) is more brightly colored than the female carpet chameleon.

Many male lizards are brightly colored. This helps them attract mates. Female lizards lay between one and fifty eggs at one time. The eggs are usually

Lizard eggs are usually soft and leathery.

soft and leathery. Some lizards give birth to live babies.

Lizards can live for many years. Geckos may live to be more than 30 years old. The Galápagos (Gah-LAH-puh-goss) land iguana has one of the longest life spans of any lizard—60 years.

From Geckos to Komodos

More than eight hundred different kinds of geckos live on Earth. Geckos have flat heads, thick tails, and scales that look like beads. They are usually less than 12 inches (30 centimeters) in length. A gecko called the Jaragua lizard is the tiniest lizard in the world. It is only 3/4 of an inch (16 mm) long!

A peacock day gecko (above) and the Jaragua lizard, the world's smallest lizard (left)

Most lizards can only hiss or growl. Geckos, however, have vocal chords. They can bark, click, or chirp. The Mediterranean gecko squeaks like a mouse.

Velcro Geckos

Geckos can zip straight up a wall and across the ceiling without falling. They can even stick to glass. This makes it easy for these night hunters to catch their favorite snacks—flies, mosquitoes, and cockroaches. What's their secret? Pads on the bottom of a gecko's toes can cling to the tiniest bumps on almost any surface—except one that is wet.

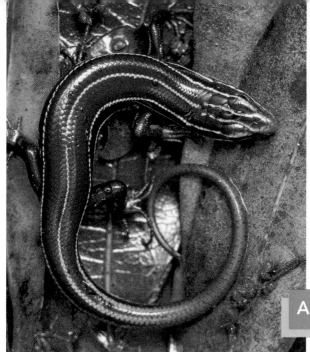

Skinks are another major group of lizards. They have pointed heads, shiny skin, heavy tails, and short legs or no legs at all.

Most skinks are less than 10 inches (25 cm) long. The five-lined skink has yellow stripes and a bright blue tail. It uses its markings to distract predators. One type of skink from New Guinea has green blood, a green tongue, and even lays green eggs.

Iguana lizards are known for their bright colors, the scales on their spines, and the crests on their heads. The green iguana can grow to be 7 feet (2 m) long.

Iguanas have pouches of skin under their throats. These are called dewlaps.

A male green
iguana inflating
its dewlap

A male iguana may inflate its
dewlap to attract a mate or
scare other males away.

A Galápagos marine iguana feeding underwater

The Galápagos marine iguana swims in the ocean. It can dive 50 feet (15 m) deep to eat seaweed.

Monitor lizards come in all sizes, from 7 inches (20 cm) to more than 10 feet (3 m) in length. They have thick necks, big claws, and strong tails. Monitors can climb, swim, and run quickly. The Komodo dragon, a type of monitor lizard, can sprint short distances at 15 miles (24 kilometers) per hour.

The Komodo dragon is the largest lizard in the world. It can grow to be 10 feet (3 m) long and can weigh 360 pounds (165 kilograms). These huge creatures live on Komodo Island and a few

The Komodo dragon is the world's largest lizard.

other small islands in Indonesia. The saliva of the Komodo carries a deadly bacteria. Komodo dragons eat pigs, monkeys, deer, other Komodos, and, rarely, humans.

Stay Away!

Lizards have many creative ways of escaping **predators**. They may use their skin color to help them blend into the background so they cannot be seen. This is called **camouflage** (CAM-uh-flawj). Desert lizards may be as white as the sand they walk on.

29

A predator would have a hard time spotting this lesser earless lizard (left). The two photos below show how a chameleon can change its skin color.

Rain-forest lizards are often green, helping them to resemble leaves. Chameleons can change color based on their mood, the amount of sunlight, or the temperature around them.

Some lizards prefer to flee from danger. Basilisk lizards rise up to run on their hind legs. They can reach speeds of up to 7 miles (11 km) per hour. Sometimes a basilisk gathers enough speed to

A basilisk lizard can race across water on its hind legs.

race across water. Special scales on the lizard's feet keep it from sinking as it skims the water's surface.

Some tree lizards float, or "fly," through the rain forest.

Skin flaps on the sides of their bodies act as "wings." The flying dragon launches into the air, spreads its flaps, and glides from one tree to the next.

A flying dragon sailing through the air

Some lizards use their decorations to protect themselves. The Jackson's chameleon scares off predators with the three large horns on its head. The thorny devil of Australia is such a prickly clump of spikes and knobs that no animal dares to bother it.

The horned lizard sprays its enemies with blood from its eyes. The Australian blue-tongued skink sticks out its bright blue tongue as a warning. The frilled lizard stands up on its

Clockwise from top left: The thorny devil, horned lizard, Jackson's chameleon, frilled lizard, and blue-tongued skink each have their own unusual way of scaring off enemies.

hind legs and flares out the ruffled collar around its neck. It will run toward its attacker, hissing and showing its bright red mouth. Lizards can put on quite a show, but most are harmless.

The Gila monster and its relative, the Mexican beaded lizard, are the only **venomous** lizards in the world. Their bites deliver liquid poison, called venom, into their prey. These venomous lizards can be found

The Gila monster has a venomous bite.

in the southwestern United
States and in Mexico. They
usually bite humans only
when they are bothered.

Tails, You Lose

A tail helps a lizard balance, walk, run, or swim. It can also come in handy when fighting off an attacker. If a predator latches on and won't let go, many lizards can snap off the ends of their tails. The tail keeps wiggling while the lizard escapes to safety. In a few weeks, a new tail will grow in its place.

A five-lined skink that has just snapped off its tail

A lava lizard with a new tail

Place in the World

Lizards help control the pest population on Earth. They eat insects and rodents that destroy valuable food crops. But many lizards are in danger of disappearing. Lizards are hunted for their meat and beautiful skins. Many lizards are taken from the wild and sold as pets.

Iguanas are the most popular reptile pet sold in the United States. More than 800,000 iguanas are taken from rain forests each year. Geckos, chameleons, and skinks are often killed because people mistakenly believe that they are poisonous.

Human development is also polluting and destroying the rain forests, grasslands, deserts, and other habitats where lizards live. In the

As rain forests (above) and deserts are destroyed, many lizards lose their natural habitats. The Texas horned lizard (right) is one type of lizard that could be in danger of disappearing.

United States, the number of Texas horned lizards has dropped because **pesticides** that humans use to protect crops are killing the ants they feed on.

Many countries are beginning to realize the importance of saving lizards. Only three thousand Komodo dragons are left in the world. Fortunately, laws now prevent them from being killed. It is also illegal to hunt Gila monsters, Mexican beaded lizards, and many other kinds of geckos and iguanas. By protecting lizards, we can make sure these ancient creatures continue to roam the Earth well into the future.

A chameleon
in Kenya

To Find Out More

Here are some additional resources to help you learn more about lizards:

Books

Barrett, Norman S. **Dragons and Lizards.** Franklin Watts, 1991.

Burns, Diane. **Snakes, Salamanders, and Lizards.** Gareth Stevens, 1998.

Miller, Sara Swan. **Snakes and Lizards: What They Have in Common.** Franklin Watts, 2000.

Richardson, Joy. **Reptiles.** Franklin Watts, 1993.

Snedden, Robert. **What is a Reptile?** Sierra Club Books for Children, 1995.

Thomas, Peggy. **Reptile Rescue.** Twenty-First Century Books, 2000.

Organizations and Online Sites

American Museum of Natural History
79th Street and
Central Park West
New York, NY, 10024
http://www.discovery.com/ exp/lizards/lizards.html

Follow along as museum scientists go on a Discovery Channel expedition to study lizards in the south-western United States.

The Nature Conservancy
4245 North Fairfax Drive, Suite 100
Arlington, VA 22203
http://nature.org

This nonprofit organization helps protect Earth's plants and animals for future generations. At this website you can learn more about endangered reptiles such as the Komodo dragon.

New England Herpetological Society
PO Box 1082
Boston, MA 02103
http://www.neherp.com

This organization works to educate the public about the importance of reptiles. Its website photo gallery features dozens of photos of lizards, snakes, and other reptiles.

Woodland Park Zoo
5500 Phinney Avenue North
Seattle, WA 98103-5897
http://www.zoo.org

Visit the website or the zoo to explore the worlds of geckos, legless lizards, skinks, and the Komodo dragon. Learn where they live, what they eat, and how they survive.

Important Words

basks warms the body by lying in the sun

camouflage the way an animal uses skin color and texture to blend in with its surroundings

ectothermic describing an animal that relies on its environment to raise and lower its body temperature

environments surroundings of living things

human development process of turning wilderness into land used by humans

keratin strong material that forms the horns, claws, nails, and scales of reptiles

pesticides chemicals used to kill insects or other pests

predators animals that hunt other animals for food

venomous able to pass venom into a victim through a bite

Index

(**Boldface** page numbers
indicate illustrations.)

Agama lizard, **9**
anole lizard, **16**
basilisk, 16, 31, **32**
blue-tongued skink, 34, **35**
brilles, 9, 10
camouflage, 29
chameleon, **10**, 11, **12, 18,
30,** 31, 34, **43**
dewlap, 24, 25
ears, 8, **9**
eating, 16, 17, **17,** 26, 28,
39
eggs, 16, 18, **19**, 24
eyes, 8, 9, 11, 34
five-lined skink, 23, **23, 38**
flying dragon, 33, **33**
frilled lizard, 34, **35**
Galápagos land iguana, 19
Galápagos marine iguana,
26, **26**
gecko, **2,** 6, 10, **10,** 19, 20,
21, **21,** 22, **22,** 40, 42
Gila monster, 16, 36, **37,** 42
glass lizard, 8, **9**
green iguana, **1,** 24, **25**

habitats, 40, **41**
horned lizard, 34, **35,** 41,
41
iguana, 7, 16, **17,** 24, 40,
42
Jackson's chameleon,
cover, 34, 35
Jacobson's organs, 12
Jaragua lizard, 20, **21**
Komodo dragon, 27, 28,
28, 42
lava lizard, **38**
legs, 8, 23, 31, 36
Mexican beaded lizard, 36,
42
molting, 15, **16**
monitors, **4,** 7, **14, 17,** 26,
27
predators, 24, 29, 34
scales, 9, 15, 20, 24, 32
skin, 15, 23, 24, 29
skinks, 7, **7,** 23, 40
tail, 8, 20, 23, 27, 38
thorny devil, 34, **35**
tongue, 11
venomous lizards, 36
yellow-headed collared
lizard, **6**

Meet the Author

Trudi Strain Trueit is an award-winning television news reporter who has contributed stories to *ABC News*, *CBS News*, and *CNN*. Ms. Trueit has written many books for Scholastic on weather, nature, and wildlife. She is the author of three other animal True Books: *Snakes*, *Turtles*, and *Alligators and Crocodiles*.

Fascinated with reptiles since her childhood, she has seen many varieties of skinks, geckos, and other lizards, including the Komodo dragon. Ms. Trueit lives in Everett, Washington, with her husband, Bill, a high-school teacher.